D0434364

Written by Guy Campbell
Illustrated by Paul Moran

Edited by Helen Brown and Sally Pilkington
With special thanks to Nicola Baxter and James Kearns
Cover design and illustration by John Bigwood
Designed by Janene Spencer

Buster Books

# Are COCONUTS More DANGEROUS Than SHARKS?

MIND-BLOWING Myths, MUDDLES & Misconceptions

Fully revised and updated edition first published in Great Britain in 2019
by Buster Books, an imprint of Michael O'Mara Books Limited,
9 Lion Yard, Tremadoc Road, London SW4 7NQ

Material in this book previously appeared in *Actually Factually*, published in 2009.

W  www.mombooks.com/buster
f  Buster Books
🐦  @BusterBooks

Copyright © Buster Books 2009, 2019
All pictures by Paul Moran, except pictures on pages 100 and 101 by Leo Broadley.

A CIP catalogue record for this book is available from the British Library.

ISBN: 978-1-78055-511-9

1 3 5 7 9 10 8 6 4 2

This book was printed in January 2019 by Leo Paper Products Ltd,
Heshan Astros Printing Limited, Xuantan Temple Industrial Zone,
Gulao Town, Heshan City, Guangdong Province, China.

# Contents

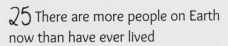

**29** Leonardo da Vinci invented the helicopter

**32** The water in your glass was once dinosaur wee

**35** We only use ten per cent of our brains

**38** Lemmings jump off cliffs

**40** No two snowflakes are identical

**42** All the vitamins in a potato are in its skin

**44** The Wright brothers invented the aeroplane

**46** Fluffy, white clouds are lighter than air

**48** Swallowed chewing gum can wrap around your organs and kill you

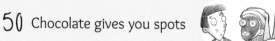

**50** Chocolate gives you spots

**52** The Sahara is the world's largest desert

**54** Wrap up warm or you'll catch a cold

**56** The Great Wall of China is the only human-made object visible from space

**58** Microwaves cook from the inside out

**61** Carrots help you see in the dark

**64** There is no gravity in space

**66** There are 24 hours in a day

**68** Global warming is caused by cows farting

**71** Pirates made people walk the plank

**73** A goldfish has a memory of about three seconds

**75** Elephants are scared of mice

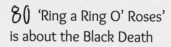

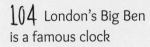 **104** London's Big Ben is a famous clock

 **106** Falling coconuts kill 15 times more people each year than sharks do

**108** Summer is warm because we are closer to the Sun

 **110** Lightning never strikes in the same place twice

**113** Hares are mad especially in March

 **115** Ostriches hide their heads in the sand

**118** The worst thing for your teeth is eating sweets

 **120** Camels store water in their humps

**123** Rats are filthy creatures

 **125** Dogs only wag their tails when they are happy

# A dog year is SEVEN human years

It is often said that every year of a dog's life is equivalent to seven years of a human's. It is true that a 14-year-old dog is pretty old for a dog, just as a 98-year-old human is pretty old for a human being.

SO IS THIS A USEFUL FORMULA?

HAPPY 21st

Dogs mature mentally and physically much faster than humans do, so a one-year-old dog is a lot more mature in dog terms than a seven-year-old child is in human terms. Aged one, a dog is almost an adult, as mature in dog terms as a human being in their teens.

During an average dog's development, the only time that the seven-years to one-year rule applies is when a dog is middle-aged. According to some experts, aged five, a dog is roughly at the same stage of maturity as a 36-year-old person.

Another reason that the formula fails is that the life span of different breeds of dog varies hugely. Mongrels (dogs that are a mix of breeds) tend to live longer than pedigree dogs (dogs with parents of the same breed).

The length of a dog's life also depends a lot on its size. Big dogs, like Great Danes, don't tend to live as long as smaller dogs. A decent innings for a Great Dane is about ten years, whereas a poodle can expect to live to around 13 years old. Some dogs have even been known to live beyond 20 years which, if this formula were true, would be over 140 for a human.

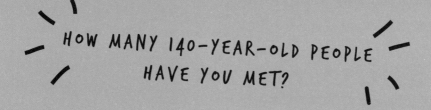

HOW MANY 140-YEAR-OLD PEOPLE HAVE YOU MET?

# Water goes down the PLUGHOLE the other way in AUSTRALIA

**No trip to the equator is complete without a real-life demonstration of this phenomenon with a water-filled bucket with a hole in the bottom.**

Tourists watch in wonder as their guide shows them the water swirling out of the bucket in one direction on one side of the equator and then swirling out the other way after they have stepped over the imaginary line. You may even have seen this demonstrated on television and, as people say, seeing is believing. OR IS IT?

The Earth is like a big ball that spins as if there is a spike passing from north to south through the centre of it. The top of this imaginary spike is called the North Pole, and the bottom of it is called the South Pole. At the equator (the imaginary line around the Earth's middle) the surface of the planet is believed to be moving at about 1,670 kilometres per hour. Further north or south from the equator the Earth's surface isn't moving as fast, and at the poles it is barely travelling at all — just gently turning.

According to scientists, this difference in the speed that the Earth's surface is moving has an effect called the 'Coriolis force'. At the equator, air moves at the same speed the Earth is turning. As this air moves north or south, it is travelling faster than the ground underneath it and begins to slow down. As it does, it turns gradually to the right if travelling north, and gradually to the left if travelling south.

The Coriolis force works slowly and takes time to occur, but it is thought that it is this force that makes weather systems, such as storms, turn clockwise in the northern hemisphere, and anti-clockwise in the southern hemisphere.

As a result, many people believe that, due to the Coriolis force, water in the southern hemisphere (the southern half of the Earth where Australia is) goes down the plughole or the toilet in an anti-clockwise direction and that in the northern hemisphere (the northern half of the Earth where the United Kingdom is located) it goes down clockwise.

This is not true. Water tends to swirl as it gurgles out of the bathtub or toilet. The way in which the water swirls can be influenced by many things, such as where the taps and plughole are positioned, how level the bathtub is and what shape it is.

While the Coriolis force is believed to cause large air masses to spin in one direction, if there was any influence on the water in your bathtub or toilet, it would be very, very small indeed.

THE TRUTH IS THAT WHETHER YOUR TOILET IS IN LONDON OR SYDNEY, THE FLUSH CAN SWIRL EITHER WAY.

# The average person swallows EIGHT SPIDERS every year while asleep

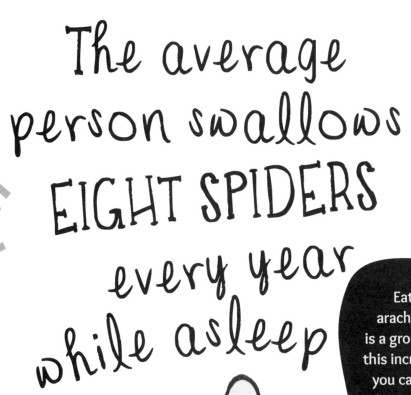

Eating eight hairy arachnids in your sleep is a gross thought, but can this incredible claim, which you can read all over the Internet, really be true?

Spiders, like most animals, don't want to be eaten and will go to great lengths to avoid it. Your average spider simply doesn't want to walk into the open mouth of a sleeping omnivore (someone who eats pretty much anything edible). Even a spider dropping down on a silken thread would take evasive action if it noticed it was heading for certain death, because it has survival instincts.

This means that to get into your mouth a spider would have to accidentally fall into it. But spiders aren't especially noted for their clumsiness. They have eight legs that make them sure-footed and agile.

However, if a spider was foolish enough to accidentally fall off a ceiling, it would need to be directly above your head and you would have to be on your back, sleeping with your mouth wide open at the precise moment it took a tumble. This is not the most common position for people to sleep in.

To then swallow the spider you would have to remain asleep, which – if a spider dropped into your mouth and started thrashing about –

SEEMS UNLIKELY.

Anyone who has swallowed even just one spider in their sleep, never mind eight, has been very unlucky indeed.

Bizarrely, the reason this 'fact' is so commonly found on the Internet, is that in 1993 a journalist called Lisa Holst wrote it in an article about all the lists of dodgy facts that can be found on the Net. She got it from an old book of common misbeliefs about insects. Her point was that some people will believe anything they find on the Internet!

# CHRISTOPHER COLUMBUS discovered America

In fourteen hundred, ninety two, Columbus sailed the ocean blue. And found this land, land of the Free, beloved by you, beloved by me.

This American poem celebrates the success of Christopher Columbus, an Italian-born explorer, known as the man who discovered what is now the USA. As a result of his achievement universities and cities have been named after him.

In fact, Columbus was not the first man to reach the USA at all. The first Americans were there over 10,000 years before Columbus arrived. Their ancestors are thought to have arrived on the American continent from Siberia, crossing over a 'bridge' of ice in the far north.

Ah, but Columbus was the first European to set foot on US soil ... wrong again. He did make four voyages and he did reach land on the western side of the Atlantic Ocean — land that became known in Europe as the New World, but at no point did he set foot in what is now known as the USA.

He is thought to have landed first in the Bahamas. He mistakenly thought he had reached India — not realizing there was a whole continent in the way. Evidence of his mistake is that he called the people he met there 'Indians'.

Even if Columbus had actually set foot in North America, he still wouldn't have been able to claim the title of the first European to visit. The Vikings (who came from Scandinavia) had set up colonies in Greenland and Canada over 400 years before he was born. There are even unproven claims that Egyptian, Chinese and Japanese ships, as well as Greek and Welsh explorers, may have landed on the continent before the Vikings.

# An insect dies after it STINGS YOU

Anyone who has been stung by a bee or a wasp might feel a little better believing that the pesky perpetrator has died a horrible death as a result of his crime. Sadly, the truth is most bees, wasps and other stinging insects can sting again and again without dying.

First of all, did you know that your armed attacker would have to be a female? With all species of wasps, bees and ants, only the female has the capacity to sting.

You may have heard that the insect will leave behind her sting when she flies off after stinging you. Not necessarily! Only a worker honeybee sometimes leaves her sting behind after using it. Her sting is barbed (which means it has lots of little hooks), so if she buries it into your fleshy arm, it can often get caught and she will have trouble flying away without leaving most of it behind. In that case, she will probably die. However, queen honeybees and most other stinging insects don't have barbed stings and suffer little hardship when they sting you.

The size of the insect that stings you doesn't dictate how badly the sting is going to hurt. It is the size of the stinger itself, how much venom it contains, and how strong the venom is, that count. For example, carpenter bees are huge – up to 25 millimetres long – but the venom in their sting is relatively feeble. Tiny fire ants, on the other hand, are only two to five millimetres long, but their sting delivers a very strong venom that can cause a huge amount of pain and discomfort.

One brave, or possibly crazy, entomologist (a person who studies insects), named Justin O. Schmidt, took it upon himself to grade insect stings according to how much they hurt. The 'Schmidt Sting Pain Index' is not a scientific scale, but it does give us an idea of which insects have the most painful stings. According to Schmidt, the most painful stings come from tarantula hawk wasps, bullet ants, velvet ants and pepsis wasps.

20

If you are ever stung by a bee, the first thing you should do is remove the sting by scraping it off. This reduces the amount of venom that can enter your body, resulting in a less painful sting. In some extremely rare cases – where a person who has been stung has an allergy to the venom – acting quickly to remove the sting and seeking medical attention can save a life.

The second thing to remember is that when bees sting, they release chemical signals called 'pheromones' into the air that tell other bees that there is danger. So once you have been stung, it is a good idea to leave the area, because reinforcements may be on the way.

# You can't find the end of a RAINBOW

Irish folk tales would have you believe that at the end of every rainbow is a leprechaun with a large crock of gold.

Unfortunately no one has ever reached the end of a rainbow to find out if this is true. This is because you can't find the end of a rainbow, right?

## WRONG!

Rainbows are the result of a marvellous trick that light performs. To see one, you need to stand with your back to the Sun on a rainy day. Light from the Sun hits a raindrop, reflects off the back wall of it and comes back out towards you. The raindrop bends the beam of light on its way in, and on its way back out, so that it leaves the drop at an angle between 40 and 42 degrees away from the angle it entered. This bending of the light is called 'refraction'.

Visible 'white' light is made up of lots of colours from violet at one end through to red at the other. This is called the 'spectrum'. These colours of light travel at different speeds. The violet light travels fastest and therefore comes out of the raindrop at 40 degrees. The red light is the slowest and leaves the drop at 42 degrees – with all the other colours in between. Each raindrop reflects a different colour, and a whole bunch of drops together reflects back a rainbow.

There are millions of colours in a rainbow, but to our eyes it looks like seven stripes of colour – red, orange, yellow, green, blue, indigo and violet – arranged in an arch shape in the sky.

BUT RAINBOWS AREN'T REALLY ARCH-SHAPED, THEY ARE CIRCULAR.

We see an arch-shaped rainbow because the ground is in the way of the bottom half of the circle. The lower the Sun is in the sky — at dawn or at the end of the day — the more of the circle you can see. The only way to see a big, almost full-circle rainbow, is if you are in a plane, looking down on the rain with the Sun above and behind you.

So if it's a circle, there can't be an end to a rainbow, can there? Well, actually there is an end to a rainbow and you don't have to trek for miles or deal with any pesky leprechauns to find it. You see, a rainbow is not physically there. You can't touch it, because it is only a trick of the light. A rainbow only exists in your eyes, or really in your brain, which receives and processes the information from your eyes. It starts as light coming from the Sun, reflects off the raindrops and comes back to your eyes as a circle of refracted light. So the 'end' of the rainbow is right inside your head.

# There are MORE PEOPLE on Earth now than have ever lived

**More people are living at this moment in time than have ever been born and died in all the years since human beings first walked on the Earth.**

It is an amazing claim, but fortunately it isn't true, because if it was, the planet would be pretty crowded.

It is thought that human beings (as we would recognize them) have been around for at least the last 50,000 years. It is impossible to work out exactly how many people have lived and died in that time, but in order to have a good guess, population experts must look at a lot of different factors. These include how many children are born each year and their life expectancy (how long each of these children can expect to live). Over the last 50,000 years, these factors have changed a lot, due to changes in peoples' living conditions, natural disasters and outbreaks of disease.

The counting of population is called a 'census', and early civilizations such as the Ancient Egyptians and the Romans performed censuses thousands of years ago to assess how many people were able to pay taxes or were fit to fight in wars. Census records have been found dating from as far back as 3,000 BC, which makes them over 5,000 years old.

These records only document limited portions of world population as the people who conducted the censuses only counted people living in their lands. However, experts at an organization called the Population Reference Bureau in Washington, DC (USA), have used these records, along with other population data, to estimate that over 108 billion people have lived and died on Earth over the last 50,000 years. The current population of the world has only recently reached 7.5 billion, and although it is true that there are more of us living now than have ever been living at any other point in history, it is very unlikely that the world's population will reach 105 billion any time soon.

# Mount Everest is the HIGHEST MOUNTAIN in the world

In almost every encyclopedia, geography textbook and book of facts that you might come across, Everest is listed as the highest mountain in the world —

## BUT NOT IN THIS BOOK.

The title of highest mountain on Earth can be awarded in a number of different ways. For example, is the highest mountain the one with the biggest distance between its bottom and its top? Or is it the one whose peak is furthest away from the centre of the planet? If that's the way we are going to measure our highest mountain, then in both cases, the highest mountain isn't Everest.

Mount Everest, which measures in at 8,850 metres, is certainly the highest point above sea level, however, that doesn't necessarily mean it is the tallest mountain in the world. The tallest mountain from base to peak is Mauna Kea in Hawaii. Mauna Kea rises just 4,205 metres above the surface of the ocean, but most of it is under water. From base to peak it measures 10,203 metres, over 1,000 metres taller than Everest.

The Earth is not perfectly round, but is what is known as an 'oblate spheroid' or, to put it another way, it is squashed like a ball that has been sat on. The Earth bulges around the middle, so the equator (the imaginary line that divides the top of the planet from the bottom of the planet, running around its middle) is approximately 22,000 metres further from the centre of the Earth than the poles are.

Mount Chimborazo in Ecuador is located very close to the equator and even though its summit is only 6,310 metres above sea level, 2,540 metres shorter than Everest, its peak is in fact over 2,000 metres further away from the centre of the Earth than Everest's.

THIS MAKES
MOUNT
CHIMBORAZO
THE HIGHEST
MOUNTAIN
IN THE WORLD.

# Leonardo da Vinci invented the HELICOPTER

**One thing that there is no doubt, is that Leonardo da Vinci, born in Italy in 1452, was a phenomenally talented man.**

He was responsible for some of the world's most famous paintings — such as the Mona Lisa. In addition to being a great artist, he was an architect, an engineer, a biologist and many other things besides.

But did da Vinci invent the helicopter? Scientists and historians have studied Leonardo's sketchbooks and notebooks and these show that he was exploring many ideas that were hundreds of years ahead of their time. For example, he drew designs for things that people today might recognize as a type of parachute, aeroplane, swing bridge and even a tank.

Some of Leonardo's designs have been made and tested in recent years and have actually worked. However, other designs were less successful.

Leonardo did design a type of helicopter in 1487. It used a giant cloth screw about four metres across. The idea was that if the screw was turned quickly, it would push enough air downwards to make the machine go up.

Instead of an engine, Leonardo's helicopter was to be powered by four men running in circles around a central shaft, turning the screw.

Unfortunately the idea, like the 'helicopter', didn't take off. Besides probably becoming very dizzy, the running men would not be able to turn the screw fast enough to get the machine off the ground. Scientists now know that Leonardo's helicopter could never work – it was too heavy to fly.

# SO WHO DID INVENT THE HELICOPTER?

The rotor-blade design used in modern helicopters was used in Chinese toys as far back as the 4th century. This is a thousand years before Leonardo was working on his man-powered chopper.

However, it was not until the internal combustion engine was invented that a helicopter could be constructed that had enough power to turn the blades fast enough to lift the machine off the ground.

It is hard to attribute the helicopter to any one inventor as there were many different designs and attempts that achieved varying levels of success. The most successful machine was probably the one invented in the USA by a Russian engineer called Igor Sikorsky.

Sikorsky's VS-300 flew for the first time on the 14th September 1939. Sikorsky later went on to develop the world's first commercial transport helicopter in the 1950's – The S-55 Chickasaw.

# The water in your glass was once DINOSAUR WEE

Has anyone ever pointed out to you that some of the water in your glass was once dinosaur wee?

## WHY WOULD ANYONE CLAIM SOMETHING THIS GROSS?

Well, it is a common belief that there is only so much water on Earth, and that it is recycled again and again. For example, water that evaporates from the ocean forms clouds, which then rain on the land, the rain pours into rivers, which then flow back into the ocean and the process begins again. The process of water changing state in this way is known as the 'water-cycle'.

Water can be frozen in an iceberg, left sitting in a puddle, or stored in a kettle waiting to be turned into a cup of tea. These are smaller cycles, but you can see the ice melt into water and evaporate, or get drunk and end up in the toilet – but the water never actually disappears.

This is why people think that there is no new water, just the same old stuff melting, evaporating and being drunk year after year. So, the water in our glass was probably once a dinosaur's wee?

Well, no. It might be possible that a one-billionth part of a glass of water may have been dinosaur wee, but the fact is that water is broken down, and new water is being made all the time. You are making new water right now. If you put a cold mirror in front of your mouth and breath out, you will notice that the mirror steams up. This is brand new water.

When you 'respire' (the chemical reaction involved in breathing), inside your body carbon, oxygen and hydrogen atoms are broken apart from one another and stuck back together as carbon dioxide and water.

All plants and animals respire in one way or another and so lots of water is created in this way.

Burning fuels, like natural gas, coal and wood, also produces new water. When fuels burn, oxygen in the air combines with carbon and hydrogen in the fuel, generating heat and also producing carbon dioxide and, yes, you guessed it, more water.

Plants actually break down water – in a process called 'photosynthesis'. They combine some of the water they take in through their roots with carbon dioxide from the air and light, and turn it all into food. So this water is being broken down and taken out of the cycle.

The chance of a water molecule that was drunk by a dinosaur surviving intact as a water molecule for millions of years and then being drunk by you is very small indeed.

# We only use TEN PER CENT of our brains

For at least a century, people have claimed that human beings use only ten per cent of their brains. It may be true that nearly two hundred years ago, scientists only understood the function of about ten per cent of a human brain. The scientists may also have believed that only ten per cent of a person's 'grey matter' was in use at any given time. THEY WERE WRONG.

Ten per cent of a human brain is made up of 'neurons' (nerve cells that are connected together). Neuron activity produces electricity and this electricity can be measured by scientists. Neuron activity is used to show which parts of a brain are in use when a person is doing different things, such as clapping, dreaming or solving puzzles.

This doesn't mean the rest of the brain isn't doing anything. The rest of the brain is made of other kinds of cells, called 'glial cells'. Glial cells are vital to the thinking and learning processes of a brain. They have important functions in maintaining and protecting neurons. The activity of glial cells is not as easy to monitor.

Today, scientists have a far greater understanding of the function of each part of the human brain. They know that you can be in a lot of trouble if even a small part of it is damaged or is not working properly. Humans use some parts of their brains for breathing, some parts for keeping their bodies at the right temperature, some parts for walking about, some for remembering things, some for solving problems and some for 'picturing' things in their heads.

But humans never use all the different parts of their brain at once. Even if a person tried to do all these things at once, they still wouldn't be using all of their brain.

Does this mean that if you could train yourself to use all of your brain at the same time, you would be incredibly clever? No – this would be impossible.

Smart people don't use more of their brains than less intelligent people. In fact, the more intelligent someone is, the less active their brain needs to be. A smart person's brain works more efficiently than that of a less smart person. It therefore requires less activity in a smaller area of the brain to complete the same task. The subject of intelligence is fascinating and new ideas about it are being developed all the time – and not with only ten per cent of scientists' brains.

## OH, AND GREY MATTER ISN'T GREY EITHER. IT'S RED.

A brain only becomes grey when it is removed from someone's head and preserved in a jar with chemicals.

# Lemmings JUMP OFF Cliffs

Lemmings are small rodents that have an alarming reputation. People believe that large groups of these cute creatures commit mass suicide by hurling themselves off cliffs to their doom.

One such sad event was famously 'captured' on camera in a Disney film called *White Wilderness* in 1958. The tragedy took place in Alberta, Canada, which in itself is strange, as it is not a place lemmings are usually found.

Further investigation of this myth reveals that for a sequence showing lemming migration, the film crew brought in a couple of crates of lemmings. The animals were made to run about for the cameras.

Then they were taken to a cliff and herded over the edge — providing an emotional ending to the film's migration story.

Ever since the movie, this image of suicidal lemmings has stuck in people's minds. But it is entirely unfair to lemmings as it just isn't true.

Some people claim lemmings commit suicide as some form of natural population control. It is true that when lemming colonies become overcrowded, large numbers may leave their burrows and head off in search of a new home where there is more food. On these journeys into the unknown, some lemmings inevitably perish attempting to swim across lakes and oceans. But they don't kill themselves on purpose.

# No two SNOWFLAKES are identical

In 1885, a man called Wilson Bentley from Jericho, Vermont (USA), combined a microscope with a camera and became the first person to photograph a snowflake successfully. He went on to capture over 5,000 images of snowflakes.

He took the pictures in order to record the beauty of the natural six-sided crystal formations we call snowflakes. And guess what? He found that of his 5,000 snowflakes, no two were exactly the same. Each flake appeared to be unique in shape.

Wilson Bentley's observation has become a popular 'fact', often repeated to describe the incredible variation that exists in nature.

# BUT IS IT TRUE?

Well, the only way someone could ever disprove this statement would be by finding two snowflakes that are identical. This might involve taking a few billion pictures and getting very lucky. Until someone does this (and no one has bothered to try yet), people will go on saying that no two snowflakes are exactly the same.

The important point here is that snowflakes are not that different from anything else. If you look hard enough, no two things are exactly the same. No two grains of sand, tennis balls or bowls of chocolate chip ice cream are exactly the same. Even identical twins are not completely 'identical'. They may look the same, but aside from having different personalities, their fingerprints are also not the same.

People and bowls of ice cream are much more complicated than snowflakes. Humans may have different numbers of freckles, or hairs on their heads and bowls of ice cream may have different numbers of chocolate chips inside them.

If you looked at a billion snowflakes, there is a good chance that a couple of them will look very similar indeed. So similar, probably, that at a quick glance you might say they were identical.

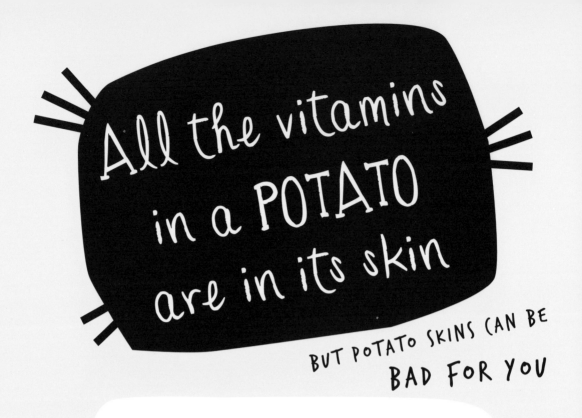

# All the vitamins in a POTATO are in its skin

## BUT POTATO SKINS CAN BE BAD FOR YOU

You have probably been told (usually by adults) that not eating the tough, leathery skin on your fluffy, buttery jacket potato is utter madness. They tell you that all the vital vitamins a potato contains are in the skin and by not eating it, you are letting the vitamins go to waste. The same is often said of apples, carrots, pears and just about anything else you might be tempted to peel.

Actually, factually, the skin of a potato is made up of dead cells and contains little in the way of health-giving vitamins. That's not all — potato skins can be bad for you. Potatoes contain toxic substances called 'glycoalkaloids' that can make you feel ill if you eat enough of them. These glycoalkaloids are found mainly in a potato's skin, especially if the potato is sprouting or a bit green.

What a potato's skin does very well, is protect the vitamins that are inside the potato from escaping when you cook it. The humble spud is a great source of many vitamins and minerals – a medium-sized one has nearly a third of the recommended daily amount of vitamin C in it – but when you fry it, bake it or boil it, a spud starts to lose its goodness fast. A peeled, boiled spud may have less than half of its vitamin C left. Leave the skin on while it is boiling, however, and nearly all that goodness stays put.

So, are there any benefits to actually eating fruit and vegetable skins? Yes, because they contain fibre. Fibre is good for you because it helps food pass through your digestive system and also lowers cholesterol levels in your blood. Some experts believe it may even reduce people's chances of developing heart disease.

# The WRIGHT BROTHERS invented the aeroplane

Most reference books will tell you that in 1903 in a town called Kitty Hawk, North Carolina (USA), Orville and Wilbur Wright made the first powered flight in an aeroplane.

THESE REFERENCE BOOKS ARE WRONG.

The Wright brothers were pipped at the post 55 years earlier by an English engineer called John Stringfellow, who worked with a partner named William Samuel Henson. They built what they called an 'aerial steam carriage' and even started a business called the Aerial Transit Company, and made plans to carry people to exotic locations all over the world.

In 1848, in an old lace factory in Somerset, England, a scale model of John Stringfellow's steam-driven aeroplane did fly – just over nine metres. Sadly, the travel business, unlike their flying machine, never got off the ground and their steam carriage never achieved sustained flight anything like that of the Wright brothers.

Stringfellow's plane was too heavy, and the steam engine wasn't powerful enough to keep it in the air for very long. It wasn't until the advent of smaller petrol-driven engines that the idea of an engine-propelled flying machine became practical.

While Stringfellow and Henson may not have achieved their dream of starting the first international airline, their plane was in the air before the Wright brothers were even born.

The British duo may not get as much credit as the Wright brothers, but theirs was certainly an incredible achievement. Replicas of their steam-driven flying machines have been exhibited around the world.

# Fluffy, white CLOUDS are lighter than air

Fluffy, white clouds slowly drifting across the sky – there is nothing nicer than lying on your back on a summer's day and looking at them, picking out their different shapes. Clouds seem to float effortlessly above our heads, so surely they must be lighter than air.

Well, let's see. When you boil the kettle, you produce water vapour. Water vapour is the invisible gas produced when water evaporates. It is the gas between the kettle's spout and the rising steam you can see. Water vapour is less dense than dry air and therefore lighter.

WELL, IF WATER VAPOUR IS LIGHTER THAN AIR, THEN CLOUDS MUST BE TOO, YES?

No. The parts of a cloud you can see aren't made of water vapour. They are made of millions upon millions of water droplets (like the steam you can see when the kettle boils). Clouds can actually weigh hundreds of tonnes and so are much heavier than air.

So how do they stay in the sky? Well, clouds start life as water vapour. Over every sea and ocean in the world, water is evaporating and turning into water vapour, which is lighter than air, and so rises. As the water vapour rises, it begins to cool and turns back into liquid water droplets. As this happens, it releases energy which makes the water droplets and the air around them warm. Warm air expands. Expanded air rises upwards because it is less dense than non-expanded air. This rising air takes the tiny droplets up with it – forming the fluffy white-looking part of a cloud. This will hang in the air until the water droplets join together and become big and heavy enough to fall out of the sky, as rain.

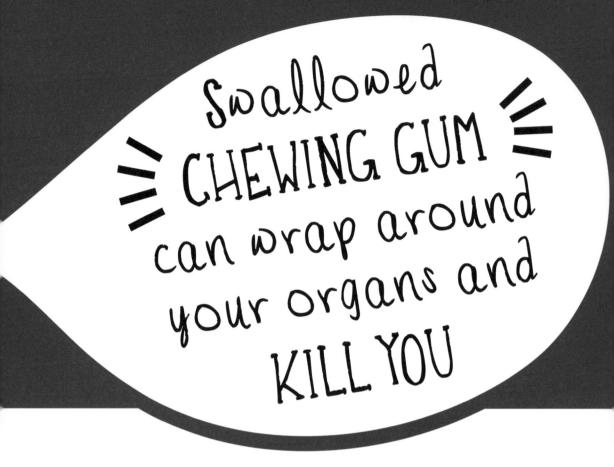

Swallowed CHEWING GUM can wrap around your organs and KILL YOU

Chewing gum is made up of chemical flavourings, sweeteners, preservatives and gum resin. All these ingredients can be digested by the human body – except the gum. So, does that mean the indigestible gum will stay in your stomach for years, eventually twisting itself around your vital organs and killing you?

No. When you eat things your body can't digest, they usually pass straight through your digestive system in a couple of days. The body moves indigestible stuff – like sweetcorn or the odd swallowed coin – along the digestive system and throws it out the other end. Only very big items sometimes get stuck along the way. So never eat ten pieces of gum and a handful of coins at once or you really will be in trouble.

That doesn't mean that swallowing chewing gum is all good news though. You can choke on a piece of gum, just as you can choke on anything else. For this reason, gum should never be given to very young children.

Sugary gum is pretty bad for your teeth, and a lot of chewing can add to wear and tear. Some artificial sweeteners have been known to cause stomach problems and other undesirable side-effects, such as diarrhoea when eaten in large quantities.

Of course, what you absolutely shouldn't do is leave chewed bits of gum squished on the pavement or anywhere else — especially in Singapore, where you can be heavily fined if you do.

# CHOCOLATE
## gives you spots

You wake up on the morning of the school disco, walk into the bathroom and look in the mirror. Disaster, an angry spot the size of a giant volcano has erupted on your once-perfect chin. You knew you shouldn't have had that bar of chocolate last night, and now you are being punished. NOT SO.

Lots of people swear that just looking at a chocolate bar will cause them to break out in 'acne' (the medical name for spots). The same goes for pizza, chips or any greasy foods. Their argument is that greasy foods must make skin greasy, and greasy skin leads to spotty skin.

It is true that the oils produced by skin, trap dirt and impurities. Dirt will block the small holes on your face called 'pores' and cause spots. But eating greasy food does not make your skin produce more oil. Your hormones increase or decrease how much oil your skin produces – not fatty foods.

'Hormones' are chemical messengers produced by glands in your body that instruct your organs to do stuff. Big changes in your body, like growing up or stress, involve lots of messages being sent to your organs telling them to change, grow, or behave differently. Hormones, not chocolate, instruct the glands that produce the oils in your skin.

Actually, factually, having some chocolate could even help fight spots. Research has shown that stress can make spots worse, and chocolate contains chemicals that can reduce stress levels in the brain and relax you.

Make-up and air pollution, meanwhile, can cause spots. Keeping your skin clean will reduce the chance of a break out. Don't try keeping it too clean as you will risk stripping your skin of oils. This will only make your skin produce more oil to replace what's missing.

Chocolate may not cause spots, but a healthy diet will help keep your skin healthy — so drink plenty of water and eat lots of fruit and vegetables to help your skin remain spotless.

# The Sahara is the world's LARGEST DESERT

A 'desert' is defined as an area of land that receives less than 250 millimetres of rain in a year. About a third of the Earth's land surface qualifies as desert under this rule.

THE SAHARA MOST CERTAINLY DOES.

The Sahara covers an area that takes up one third of the whole African continent — over 8.6 million square kilometres. This is not much smaller than the size of the USA.

## SO THE SAHARA IS THE WORLD'S LARGEST DESERT, RIGHT?

Wrong. It is the world's third largest desert, after the Antarctic at number one, covering up to 18 million square kilometres in winter, and the Arctic at number two, covering about 15 million square kilometres in winter. Even though these areas are icy wastelands, and not the kind of places you would usually think of when the word 'desert' is mentioned, their low average rainfall qualifies them as deserts, and both are substantially bigger than the Sahara.

But doesn't that mean that the Arctic is an ocean and a desert at the same time? Well, yes it does, but that's science for you!

# Wrap up warm or you'll catch a COLD

You are running out the door to meet some mates at the park and some interfering adult makes you put on six jumpers, a coat and a scarf so big you can barely walk let alone catch a Frisbee, so you won't catch a cold. Does this sound familiar?

If you dress up like a woolly mammoth you won't catch a cold, right?

# WRONG. COLDS AND FLU ARE CAUSED BY VIRUSES, NOT BY LOW TEMPERATURES.

Viruses are chemical packages – not living things like bacteria. Viruses use the cells inside our bodies to multiply and spread, but they aren't particularly affected by cold weather or how many layers of clothing you wear.

So why do cold and flu bugs seem to thrive in the winter months? There isn't really a proven answer to this question, but there are a few theories to think about. Here are some of them:

- In winter time, people tend to stay indoors with the windows closed. Being indoors means people are closer together and more likely to pass on their germs. In addition, a warm environment is perfect for bugs to live and breed in.

- If you ever get really, really cold, you can suffer from a condition called 'cold stress'. Cold stress lasts for a few days and can include a runny nose and shivering. You don't have a virus, but some of the symptoms look and feel the same.

- The shorter days and colder temperatures in winter can make human beings miserable and stressed. It is dark, wet and cold, and we aren't running around in the sunshine. Stress and depression can lower our resistance to illness and make us more likely to catch a cold.

# The GREAT WALL OF CHINA is the only human-made object visible from space

The Great Wall of China is a pretty amazing construction. It is a wall that today stretches a total of 2,400 kilometres, and was begun over 2,200 years ago by the Chinese Emperor Shi Huandi, to protect his empire from invaders. What's even more amazing is that something built that long ago can actually be seen from modern spacecraft. Unfortunately for the wall, it isn't the only human-made thing an astronaut can admire from space.

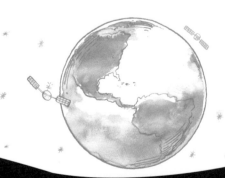

The nearest bit of
'space' isn't really that
far away from the Earth's
surface. A very low orbit for a
spaceship would only be about 200 kilometres above the
Earth. From this height, parts of the Great Wall are visible, but so are
some roads, airports, buildings and even the Great Pyramids of Egypt.

The truth of the statement also depends on what is considered a
'human-made' object. There are things that stand out far more than
the Great Wall, such as cities or reservoirs, which are created by people.

Is the Great Wall of China the only man-made thing visible from
the Moon? The Moon is nearly 400,000 kilometres from Earth, and
according to astronauts who have been there, all you can see of the
Earth is a beautiful sphere, with white clouds, blue patches of ocean
and areas of yellow and green land.

The only human-made objects that an astronaut standing on the Moon's
surface would see are satellites and the spacecraft they arrived in.

# Microwaves cook from the INSIDE OUT

Anyone who has warmed up an apple pie in a microwave knows that while the outside pastry feels cool to the touch, the inside can be the temperature of molten lava — capable of burning the skin off your tongue in three thousandths of a second. But do microwave ovens cook food from the inside out?

It is true that microwaves work differently from ordinary ovens, which cook food from the outside in. An ordinary electric or gas oven fills up with heat. Anything inside eventually warms up too, as the heat passes into it. The longer an apple pie is in the oven, the deeper the heat will penetrate it. The middle of the pie will be the last part to get warm. The air inside the oven is also hot and dry, which means the outside of the pie can go crisp and eventually burn.

Microwaves don't heat up the air inside them. They use a type of radio wave, unsurprisingly known as a 'microwave'. These microwaves are emitted by a 'magnetron' inside the microwave and are absorbed mainly by water molecules.

When microwaves are absorbed by the water molecules in food, the molecules begin to shake vigorously and heat up. If you think of the food in your microwave as being made of layers, each about one centimetre thick, the first layer absorbs ten per cent of the microwaves, leaving 90 per cent for the next layer. This layer also absorbs another ten per cent, and so on, leaving even less of the original radiation for the layers underneath. So technically microwaves cook from the outside in, too.

However, as microwaves are absorbed particularly well by water molecules, if the food you are cooking is something that contains more water on the inside than the outside, such as a potato, or indeed an apple pie, then the inside of the food will get hotter quicker than the outside.

If the food you are heating is something that has pretty much the same amount of water all the way through, such as a lump of cheese, the outside will heat very slightly earlier than the inside. This is because the microwaves reach the outer areas first as they pass through it.

This is why, on the packaging of microwaveable food, you are advised to allow a 'stand time'. After the microwave oven containing your apple pie has gone 'ping', you leave the pie to stand for a minute, while the lava-hot middle transfers some of its heat to the cool outer pastry. Hey presto, you have a more evenly warmed dessert that won't leave you 'thpeaking like thith'!

# CARROTS help you see in the DARK

Everybody knows that vegetables are good for you, and carrots are no exception. Carrots contain a healthy dose of vitamin A (from beta-carotene), which helps your body to grow, resist infections, and keeps your skin and bones in good condition, all the while maintaining good eyesight. But can eating carrots really give you the amazing ability to see in the dark?

Actually, factually, no. While vitamin A is essential to healthy vision, consuming lots of it doesn't make your vision any better, or help you to see in the dark. In a study conducted in Australia for a television programme, Dr Andrew Rochford ate 15 kilograms of carrots over ten days and measured whether his ability to see in dimly lit conditions improved. It didn't — not even a little bit.

So how did a humble orange vegetable get such an incredible reputation for improving eyesight? Well, you can blame the British Royal Air Force.

One week during the Second World War – while Britain was under constant threat of bombing raids from the German air force – the number of enemy planes being shot down by British pilots suddenly showed a remarkable increase.

The British government spread the rumour that RAF pilots had been put on a scientifically approved high-carrot diet to improve their night vision. The newspapers published stories about pilots like John 'Cats' Eyes' Cunningham, whose apparent ability to see in the dark and shoot down enemy planes at night was put down to his love of carrots.

In reality there wasn't any truth behind the story — it was a carefully constructed lie. The British had developed a new radar system — Airborne Interception Radar, otherwise known as AI — that allowed them to locate German planes from much further away. Enemy bombers were tracked and intercepted more easily by British fighter planes, so consequently many more were shot down before they could drop their bombs.

The British made up the carrot story to cover up their new invention. But ever since, the humble carrot has kept its reputation as a magical aid to night vision.

# There is NO GRAVITY in space

We have all seen pictures of astronauts floating around weightlessly in spaceships. They bounce off the walls. Anything that is not nailed down floats around with them. This is because there is no gravity in space, right?

Actually, factually, no. Gravity (a force that pulls objects towards each other) is everywhere, including space. Gravity keeps the Moon close to the Earth. It makes the Earth orbit the Sun, rather than just drifting about in space and getting cold.

## SO WHY DO ASTRONAUTS FLOAT AROUND?

The gravitational pull of the Earth pulls a spaceship downwards, so that it is falling. However, because the spaceship is travelling very fast, it does not fall down to Earth. Instead, it falls into a circular orbit around the Earth.

Astronauts are falling, too, but the speed at which the spacecraft is travelling acts against the pull of gravity. The astronauts inside are perfectly balanced between being thrown out into space and falling to the Earth – so they float in mid-air.

The further away something gets from Earth, the less effect Earth's gravity has on it. At about 500 kilometres up, where a spacecraft might be orbiting, the effect of gravity on an astronaut is roughly about 15 per cent less than it is on the ground. This means he or she would weigh about 15 per cent less than they do on Earth. Even though they might feel lighter than air as they bob around in the space shuttle, astronauts aren't 'weightless' at all.

# There are 24 HOURS in a day

When everything else is being called into question it is nice to be able to rely on the fact that there are 24 hours in a day. It is a truth so reliable you can set your alarm clock by it. Or is it?

Well, it depends on how a day is defined. People often define a day as the amount of time it takes for the Earth to complete one rotation on its axis. This is the amount of time it takes for the Sun to reach the same point in the sky. There are 24 hours between noon today and noon tomorrow.

But this doesn't mean there are 24 hours in a day, because the Earth also orbits the Sun once a year. This has the effect of cancelling out one of the Earth's daily spins per year, and brings the average length of a day nearer to 23 hours 56 minutes.

However, this doesn't mean that every day is
23 hours 56 minutes long. The Earth's orbit of the Sun
is not perfectly circular. It is more like an oval. So the Earth
is closer to the Sun at some points during its orbit than at
other times. When it is closer to the Sun, the Earth travels
a bit faster due to the pull of the Sun's gravity. When it is
further away, this gravitational effect is weaker, so the Earth
travels a bit slower. This change in speed has the effect of
making some days longer than others, but an average day
works out at 23 hours 56 minutes long.

To make sure we are keeping good time with the Sun, we
add an extra day (29th February) once every four years.
We call this a 'leap year'.

However, the correction made by adding one day every four
years is just a bit too much. It would make us gain about
three days every 400 years. To make up for this, at the end
of every century, we miss a leap year out, unless the year
can be divided by four hundred.

GULP!

# Global warming is caused by cows FARTING

Scientists are in overwhelming agreement that the world is getting warmer, and this is at least partly due to the 'greenhouse effect'. The greenhouse effect is caused by increasing levels of gases called 'greenhouse gases' in the Earth's atmosphere. Greenhouse gases include carbon dioxide, ozone and methane. These gases form a layer around the Earth and prevent heat from the Sun escaping back out into space. As this layer grows thicker, less and less heat is allowed to escape and the planet becomes warmer.

HOW IS THIS THE COWS' FAULT, YOU MIGHT ASK?

Cows produce methane. Lots of methane. A single cow can produce over 200 litres of methane in a single day. Cows eat hay and grass, which are very hard to digest. They have special microbes in their stomachs that help to break them down and these microbes produce methane as they do this. The cows then release this methane into the atmosphere.

Increasing demand for beef and dairy products has meant that cow numbers have been increasing rapidly over the past 50 years. It is estimated that there are now over a billion cows on the planet. Scientists are so concerned with the amount of methane the cows are producing that they are working on antibiotics to add to cow feed that will stop the microbes making so much gas.

SO, COWS' FARTS DO CAUSE GLOBAL WARMING?

No. The 200 litres of methane per cow actually comes out as burps, not farts. In order to digest their food, cows need to 'regurgitate' or sick-up food they have swallowed back into their mouths and chew it over again. This is called 'chewing the cud'. As cows do this, they release methane gas into the atmosphere.

Cows' burps do contribute to global warming but they are certainly not the only cause, and even then it is not the cows' fault but ours because of our growing appetite for beef and dairy products.

Greenhouse gases are produced in many other ways, not just by cows. Burning fossil fuels like coal and gas in power stations, using petrol in our cars, and burning large areas of rainforest all release massive amounts of carbon dioxide into the atmosphere.

# PIRATES made people walk the plank

**Pirates don't have the best of reputations. If you imagine a pirate you probably picture a bloodthirsty cut-throat, with one eye, a wooden leg and a parrot on his shoulder, making prisoners walk the plank.**

A couple of these fearsome attributes are probably accurate — sailing was a dangerous job and the odd eye and leg went missing in action. However, most of this image of ruthless outlaws has been created by the writers of storybooks and Hollywood films.

Ships carrying cargo across the seas were often poorly armed. They didn't have the weapons needed to put up a fight against a band of approaching pirates armed to the teeth. Sailors were badly paid and usually surrendered not long after the pirates' well-armed ship came into view.

Generally, pirates loaded stolen goods on to their own ship and allowed the vanquished vessel and its crew to go free unharmed. It was useful for pirates to have a scary reputation, so people didn't dare resist them. In reality, they didn't kill people very often.

Pirates probably didn't have parrots, either. A lot of ships had a cat to keep the rat population down, but a parrot? Robert Louis Stevenson's book, *Treasure Island*, may have been responsible for this one.

What about walking the plank? Prisoners walk the plank in almost every pirate film ever made. There is no record of pirates ever making people do this. For a start, ships didn't have 'planks' — a pirate captain wishing to punish a prisoner was much more likely just to have pushed him over the side.

The plank legend may go back to the Roman historian Plutarch who lived during the first century AD. He wrote about the pirates of that era. When boarding a victim ship, they would single out any Romans on board and grant them their freedom — by letting them climb down the ship's ladder into the open sea.

# A goldfish has a MEMORY of about three seconds

This goldfish 'fact' is a comforting belief. It makes you feel much better about keeping your fishy friend in a little glass bowl with just a plastic castle and some coloured gravel for company. If a goldfish has a memory that short, it won't get bored. Every time the fish does a lap of the bowl, it will be like a whole new world to them.

Unfortunately for your peace of mind and for the fish, goldfish are smarter than you think, and have memories a lot longer than three seconds. In scientific tests, goldfish have learned to swim through mazes and perform the odd trick for food. They have been able to remember how to repeat what they did up to 11 months later. This is said to be the equivalent of a human remembering something for over 40 years.

Further evidence of a good memory comes when a goldfish sees an unfamiliar human. Fish that normally swim about and play with each other can become very shy when a stranger enters the room in which their bowl is standing. They will hide at the back of the bowl or behind that plastic castle.

Fish can also be wary of being fed by strangers, whereas they might take food straight from the hand of a person they are familiar with. Amazingly, cases have been studied where a blind goldfish can recognise the voice of its owner and tell it apart from the voice of a stranger.

So get your goldfish a couple of fishy buddies and a bigger bowl to swim around in – it isn't as dumb as you might think!

# Elephants are scared of MICE

It sounds crazy considering their size, but time after time you will see cartoons of elephants jumping on the nearest chair at the sight of a mouse, quivering like jelly and crying like a baby.

## BUT WHY WOULD AN ELEPHANT BE SCARED OF A MOUSE?

Some people have suggested that it is because mice are small enough to crawl up an elephant's trunk and that this could cause them to suffocate. However, this would mean an elephant would be scared of lots of other small animals. Also, an elephant could blast a mouse out of its trunk if it wanted to. Moreover, why would a mouse want to go up there in the first place?

A more believable explanation of the theory involves an
elephant's eyesight. Elephants don't have the greatest eyesight
in the world, and while they tend to be pretty fearless when
it comes to large animal threats such as lions, they can get
spooked when they hear something that they can't see. A
mouse scrabbling about an elephant's feet could make an
elephant nervous until they can actually see what it is.
Then they are likely to relax again.

A particularly unscientific experiment carried out on an American television show seems to support this theory. A mouse was hidden under a dried piece of elephant dung. When an elephant approached, the dung was pulled out of the way revealing the mouse. The elephant was startled and got out of the way pretty quickly. However, when they tried the experiment again, the elephant wasn't startled and didn't run away, even though it avoided the mouse. This behaviour suggests elephants hate surprises, but not necessarily mice.

One small animal that elephants do seem to be scared of is the bee, or rather lots of bees. Despite elephants' thick hides, bees can sting them around the eyes and up their trunks, which can cause them a lot of discomfort. Studies in Kenya have found that not only will elephants flee from bees, but they will also steer clear of audio speakers playing the sound of bees. Research is being done to see if this 'apiphobia' (fear of bees) can be used by Kenyan farmers to protect their crops from invading elephants. It is thought that a fence made of beehives could make crop-crushing elephants buzz off!

# Bats are BLIND

You will have heard the expression 'as blind as a bat', probably when you were desperately searching for something that a 'helpful' friend points out was right in front of you all along.

## BUT ARE BATS REALLY ALL THAT BLIND?

Bats come out at night and are able to find their way in the dark. Brilliant eyesight would be wasted on any animal that only went around in the dark. Bats also have really big ears. Brilliant hearing would help to make up for not being able to see very well.

However, while it is true that bats do have excellent hearing, most of them also happen to have pretty good eyesight. Some bats have eyesight that is better than that of us humans.

Bats are used to living in the dark — spending their time hanging around in large, pitch-black caves. They have an amazing system called 'echolocation' to help them get around. A bat squeaks and the sound of the squeak bounces off things and the bat picks up the echoes.

This is a bit like the sonar systems scientists have developed for finding things under water, but the bats' system is much, much better.

By squeaking and listening to the echo, a bat builds up an incredibly detailed picture of what is around it. It can use echo to locate exactly where a tiny insect is hovering. The picture the bat builds up in its mind as it flies also gives it a 'map' that it can use to get back home when it has finished hunting.

This echolocation system is more useful to the bat than simply using its eyesight, allowing it to gather more information quickly. For that reason, some bats' eyesight is not very highly developed, but no species of bat is actually blind.

# 'Ring a Ring O' Roses' is about the BLACK DEATH

Ring a ring o' roses
A pocket full of posies
Atishoo, atishoo
We all fall down.

You may have sung this nursery rhyme in the playground, circling round, hand-in-hand and eventually falling to the ground. But did you know that people say the rhyme was written about the Black Death?

The Black Death, the name given to a massive outbreak of bubonic plague, swept through Europe between 1347 and 1353. It killed over one third of Europe's total population. Some historians date the rhyme back to this period, others date it later, to the Great Plague of London in 1665. They associate the rhyme with outbreaks of plague because they believe the words describe the symptoms of the disease.

Along with a fever and being generally very ill, a sufferer of the plague would develop 'buboes', swellings the size of eggs, around their groin and armpits. These swellings would eventually lead to red marks on their skin (*rosy rings*). Victims sneezed (*Atishoo, atishoo*), and in 70 per cent of cases, they died (*We all fall down*). So many people died of bubonic plague, that people carried small bouquets of flowers (*A pocket full of posies*) with them, to cover up the smell of disease and rotting bodies.

However, the earliest written record of *'Ring a Ring O' Roses'* comes from a book published in 1881, over 500 years after the Black Death. It is possible that no one wrote the rhyme down for 500 years, but this is unlikely, because nursery rhymes were a popular subject for books many years before 1881. Also, while the words of the rhyme do fit the symptoms of the disease perfectly, there are lots of other versions of the rhyme from different countries around the world. In many of these versions the words of the rhyme are completely different and have no connection with sneezing or red marks.

It wasn't until the 1950s that someone suggested in their book that the rhyme might have something to do with the Black Death. The idea seemed so deliciously gruesome – kids were skipping around singing about this horrible killer disease – that the connection has been accepted as 'fact' ever since.

# Heat RISES

If you have ever seen steam rising from a boiling kettle, watched the shimmering air above a hot road, or witnessed a hot-air balloon lifting into the sky, you can't be blamed for coming to the conclusion that heat rises.

Except that it doesn't. Heat actually travels from anywhere that's hot to anywhere that's less hot. This can happen in any direction, not necessarily up. When you heat something, you make the molecules in it move around. In turn, those molecules knock into the other molecules making them move around, too. This is how heat spreads through stuff and it is called 'conduction'.

You see, or rather feel, conduction at work when you heat a block of metal. It doesn't matter if the block is heated at the top or the bottom or even from one side, the heat spreads evenly in every direction, not specially upwards.

The truth is (and this might sound like cheating) hot stuff, such as air or water, does tend to rise. For example, when the air molecules in a hot-air balloon are heated, they move around and get further apart. This causes the air inside to expand. It makes the air inside the balloon less dense than the air outside. So it is this hot air that causes the balloon to rise, not the heat itself.

HOT AIR RISES. HOT WATER RISES, BUT HEAT DOESN'T RISE ON ITS OWN!

# BEARS hibernate

In old cartoons, as winter approaches, bears put on their pyjamas, make their beds and set their alarm clocks for spring. It is hibernation time and they do not wish to be disturbed. In these cartoons, the bears aren't usually allowed to sleep for long – they are woken up by chipmunks and beavers throwing nuts or noisily chopping down trees nearby.

For a lot of creatures, including bears, the winter months can be harsh. Food is a lot harder to come by, and they require more energy to keep warm in the cold temperatures.

A good way of making the winter months pass by faster is to curl up somewhere warm and cosy and sleep. Bears do this. To help save their energy, their heartbeats slow down and so does their breathing. Their bodies survive on reserves of fat built up in the autumn. When spring comes around, bears are very hungry indeed and a lot thinner than they were when they went to sleep.

ISN'T THAT HIBERNATING?

No. Even though a sleeping bear is saving energy by breathing more slowly, it is still using energy up keeping warm. The real hibernators, like hedgehogs, groundhogs and bats, go a little further.

The bodies of hibernating animals get much colder. The blood temperature of a hibernating groundhog (a kind of rodent found in North America) can drop to just a couple of degrees above freezing. Four breaths happen every minute and its heart beats only once every 15 seconds. The groundhog's brain activity almost stops, and it is as close to dead as it can be. A hibernating groundhog is using 90 per cent less energy than a sleeping bear and so it can stay like this for up to eight months without eating.

It is also almost impossible to wake a hibernating groundhog up. A pesky chipmunk could shout in its ear and nothing would happen. Shout in the ear of a sleeping bear on the other hand, and you will have a very awake, very hungry and very angry bear to deal with.

# Tutankhamun's tomb was CURSED

In November 1922, archaeologist Howard Carter's seven-year quest to find the tomb of an 18-year-old pharaoh, known as Tutankhamun, came to an end. As he stood before an ancient stone door that bore the crest of the boy king, Carter sent for his financial backer, Lord Carnarvon, to join him to wonder at the priceless treasures within.

According to newspaper reports at the time, a chilling curse was found inside the tomb.

*Death shall come on swift wings to Him that touches the Tomb of the Pharaoh*

Many people believe that this curse wreaked havoc amongst archaeologists and museum staff long after the tomb's discovery.

The tomb had lain undisturbed for over 3,000 years. After discovering the stone door, it took Carter and his men three months to reach the inner room that contained Tutankhamun's mummified body encased in three coffins, one inside the other. The innermost coffin was made of solid gold.

Barely two weeks after laying eyes on Tutankhamun, Lord Carnarvon was dead. The world's newspapers, already stirred up by the discovery of the tomb and its treasures, went crazy at the idea of 'The Curse of King Tut'. Over the next few years, stories of its dark influence spread. Some suggested that up to 26 people involved with the expedition had died prematurely since the tomb's discovery.

Tutankhamun's treasures went on a world tour, and when employees at museums in New York and Paris died shortly after the exhibitions, the press concluded that the curse was following the king's remains. The tomb's fabulous artefacts still tour the world today, and the curse rumours follow them wherever they go.

The truth is that there was no curse found in Tutankhamun's tomb. A journalist made it up. Lord Carnarvon did die of pneumonia two weeks after seeing Tutankhamun's mummy, but he had been in pretty poor health for years.

Six people who were involved in the discovery of the tomb did die within ten years of its opening, but ten years is quite a long time, and some of the people were quite old. The vast majority of those present at the opening lived long and healthy lives. Howard Carter, himself, lived to be 64, and if anyone was going to be cursed, it should surely have been him.

Dozens of books and films have kept the idea of King Tut's curse alive. But, happily, there is no evidence that contact with Tutankhamun, or his artefacts, will shorten your life. So if you should ever have the opportunity to see these incredible treasures for yourself – go!

# NAPOLEON
## was short

When people say that someone has a 'Napoleon complex,' they are actually saying that a person is particularly short and bossy. But is this a fair way for Napoleon Bonaparte to be remembered?

Napoleon was born in Corsica in 1769. He must have been quite bossy from an early age if his success is anything to go by. He was a soldier in the French army and, due to his incredible leadership skills and battle strategy, he rose quickly through the ranks.

He was leading the entire army by the age of 30, and eventually declared himself Emperor of France. Napoleon fought and won many battles and is widely believed to have been one of the world's finest military leaders.

Aside from his outstanding military abilities, the other thing Napoleon is famous for is being short. But just how short was he?

The simple answer to this is that he was not particularly short compared to other people at the time (people were generally a bit shorter back then).

## SO WHY DO WE KNOW HIM NOW AS BEING SHORT?

There are a few reasons why he may have got this reputation. Firstly, his nickname in France was 'le petit caporal'. Directly translated this means 'the little corporal' but in fact, the French also use the word 'petit' to mean 'special'. Napoleon was a general, a much higher rank than a corporal, but they called him 'the special corporal' to show that he was a friend to ordinary soldiers, not a big shot general who only hung out with other generals.

Another reason Napoleon may have appeared short was because of his elite guard (the soldiers who protected him personally). These men were generally over six feet tall – unusually tall for the time – and at least half a foot taller than him. So walking amongst them he must have looked rather small, even though he was of average height.

Thirdly, Napoleon gained the reputation of being short due to a miscalculation of his height. In the eighteenth century, the French system of measuring was different to that used in Britain. A French inch was longer than a British inch. So, although it is often written that Napoleon was five feet and two inches in French measurements, in British measurements this would have been five feet and six inches, which makes him 168 centimetres tall.

Lastly, it would have suited the rest of Europe to believe that Napoleon was short. His armies were feared throughout the continent. Anything that made the French general seem a bit less scary would have been seized upon by his enemies – like making out he was a titch. But they probably wouldn't have said it to his face ...

# HEINZ has 57 varieties

Everyone has heard of Heinz, the huge food manufacturer selling millions of tins of soup and baked beans, bottles of tomato ketchup and other products all over the globe. Their labels boast that there are 57 different varieties of Heinz products available.

Actually, there are more than 57 varieties of Heinz food ...

## ... MANY, MANY MORE – THOUSANDS IF YOU COUNT ALL THE DIFFERENT RECIPES AVAILABLE FROM COUNTRY TO COUNTRY.

Henry John Heinz started selling his bottled pickles and vegetables in 1869. He was a success from the start, putting his pickles in clear glass bottles so the customers could see what they were getting. To draw attention to his products, he started putting massive advertising 'pickles' all over America, including a giant 12-metre long flashing pickle that lit up New York City as part of a sign six floors high.

Mr Heinz's advertising campaigns were a huge success, and so was his company. He expanded his range to include lots of other canned and bottled foods.

So then why do people say there were 57 varieties? Well, in the 1890s Mr Heinz spotted a poster for a shoe company advertising 21 different styles. The precise number appealed to him. At the time, he was already selling more than 57 varieties of products, but he felt the numbers five and seven were special and lucky for him and his wife. So he chose 57 and stuck with it.

To this day, the labels on Heinz products carry the number 57, and a little picture of a pickle, too. Take a look for yourself the next time you see a can of Heinz Baked Beans.

# Your body is as OLD as you are

On your last birthday you might have turned eight or 12, or 109 years old. But if you think your body is actually any of those ages, you are mistaken.

Your body is in fact lots of different ages because it is constantly mending and replacing worn out bits of itself. Red blood cells, for example, last an average of only four months before the body replaces them with bright, shiny new ones.

Until recently, scientists were unsure about how often the human body replaces different cells. New research, however, has enabled them to measure the age of cells much more accurately. They now know the cells that make up your stomach lining are replaced with new ones every five days or so. The cells that make up your liver are replaced roughly every 18 months, and the muscles in your chest are replaced about every 15 years. Even the cells in your bones are replaced. It is thought that your body is able to replace your entire skeleton over a period of about ten years.

So, even if you are 109 years old, there may be no part of your body that is actually 109. Your eyes, bones, stomach, liver, kidneys, etc, are all much younger than that. In fact, if the average age of all the different cells that make up an adult's body was worked out, it would be between seven and ten years old.

If all this is true and a body regenerates itself over and over again, why can't humans live forever? Because as people get older their bodies get less efficient at replacing cells and this makes people more at risk of wear and tear.

Medical science hasn't found a way to help people live forever, but the scientists studying cells might one day make exciting medical breakthroughs that really will help us to live longer.

# Cut a worm in half, and you get TWO WORMS

When you are digging in the garden and your spade chops a worm in half, it might make you feel better to believe that one worm will become two worms and wiggle off unharmed by the experience. But this might not be the case for your worm victim.

Earthworms do have a remarkable ability to lose parts of their bodies and grow them back again (or just live without them). If grabbed by a bird, say, some worms have the ability to 'eject' their tails. The bird will fly off with a small part of the tail, while the worm escapes with its life.

But it is not accurate to say that you get two worms if you cut one in half. What you are likely to get is either one dead worm in two halves, or one worm that is half as long as it used to be.

Worms are simple creatures. They have no eyes, no ears, no nose, no lungs and get by with very few organs inside their bodies. They do, however, have hearts — in fact, five hearts. All of these are located near a worm's head. If you cut a worm in half, the hearts will not be able to supply blood to the tail end of the worm and that part will quickly die.

The bottom half of a worm is made of basic fatty tissue, which the worm's body can repair and replace. The five hearts and other major organs in the top half of a worm are more complicated. If they are damaged or removed, the worm cannot replace them. It's a bit like when you nibble at the skin around your fingers, it grows back, but if you chewed your whole arm off, it wouldn't!

# Chameleons change COLOUR to match their background

It would make a lot of sense for chameleons to use their amazing ability to change colour as a way of camouflaging or hiding themselves from predators looking for a light lizardy lunch. It would make sense, but they can't and they don't.

For one thing, a chameleon has a limited number of colours it can be. If one was sitting against a background that was, say, purple, try as the chameleon might, nothing could make it turn purple.

Chameleons have four layers of skin that reflect light. These layers of skin are made of cells that contain different-coloured pigments. By changing the size of the colour cells in these layers, some chameleons can produce black, white, blue, yellow, green and red colour-combinations.

So why do chameleons change colour? It depends on how they feel. It is all about their mood, rather than their environment. Chameleons change colour when they are stressed, angry, hot, scared or just relaxed. Studies have also shown that chameleons can communicate using colour, displaying messages like 'You are one cute chameleon', or 'Back off!'

Colour changes vary according to species, too. Some chameleons don't change colour at all.

Not all angry chameleons are the same colour, but once you get to know one, you should be able to tell what mood it's in just by looking at it.

IF ONLY PEOPLE WERE AS EASY TO READ ...

# You SHOULD be afraid of the big bad wolf

We are taught as kids to be wary of wolves. Fairy tales such as *Little Red Riding Hood* and *The Three Little Pigs* portray wolves as devious characters whose only aim is to gobble you up. Dressing up as your grandma, blowing down your house — no trick is too low for a sneaky wolf, hungry for human (or little piggy) flesh.

# BUT ARE WOLVES REALLY DANGEROUS TO HUMAN BEINGS?

Wolves are big, strong and fast animals, with sharp teeth. If they wanted to eat people, they could, very easily. But the truth is that while wolves will certainly attack pigs or sheep, they will do whatever they can to avoid being in the position of having to attack a human being.

Wolves avoid people whenever they can. Wild wolves will do their best to keep at least half a kilometre between themselves and people. This means that seeing a wolf is a very rare occurrence.

Mind you, if you do see a wolf it isn't a good idea to approach it with a friendly pat on the head. You should make as much noise as possible to scare it away. The only reason that wolves are not a threat to humans is because they are scared of us. Wolves that are used to being around people and living alongside them lose some of their fear. This is when very rare attacks can occur.

In North America and Canada, where wild wolves are known to live, there have been very few reported cases of people having been injured by wolves, let alone having been killed and eaten by them.

You are much more likely to be knocked over by a lightning-fast grandma than attacked by a wolf, and several thousand times more likely to be attacked by her pet dog.

# London's BIG BEN is a famous clock

Big Ben is not just a famous clock, but one of the most famous clocks in the world. People all around the world who see a picture of Big Ben will recognize it instantly and think of London, where the clock sits at the top of Elizabeth Tower (previously named Saint Stephen's Tower), which forms part of the Houses of Parliament.

Actually, that is all wrong. The Houses of Parliament are actually called the 'Palace of Westminster', and Big Ben is not the clock, but the name of the largest of the five bells that are part of the clock.

So Big Ben is a bell — that's not very exciting. Well, it depends on how you look at it. The bell isn't just big. At the time it was made, it was the biggest bell ever and was going to form part of one of the most accurate clocks in the world. It was so big that it took 20 days to pour molten metal into the mould, and a further 20 days for it to cool.

The bell weighs 13.7 tonnes, which is as much as four elephants. A bell that big is very difficult to make, so people weren't very happy when the first one cracked when it was tested. The hammer used to hit it was too big.

Another bell had to be made, but it cracked after two months. This time, rather than replace the very expensive bell again, it was turned round so the crack was on the other side from the hammer and the big hammer was replaced by a smaller one. To this day, the 'bong' made by Big Ben is slightly out of tune because of the crack.

Now you know why the bell is called 'Big', but why 'Ben'? It was either named after a huge bare-knuckle boxer of the time, Ben Caunt, or after a politician, also huge, called Sir Benjamin Hall. The real story is probably a little of both.

# Falling coconuts KILL 15 times more people each year than sharks do

This statistic is quoted all the time in news articles and on websites and aims to show people why, despite many scary films, they shouldn't be afraid of sharks –

## BUT IS IT REALLY TRUE?

Approximately five people are killed by sharks each year. This is not as many as you might think, considering there are over 7.6 billion people in the world and most of them are terrified of sharks.

For this 'fact' to be true, on average 75 people must be killed a year by falling coconuts. Should you be terrified of coconuts? Why doesn't Steven Spielberg make a scary film about killer coconuts on the rampage?

## BECAUSE IT SIMPLY ISN'T TRUE.

While coconuts can be heavy (up to a couple of kilograms) and the trees they grow on can be pretty tall (up to 25 metres), there is no evidence that they are killing 75 people a year.

Coconuts are very securely attached to a tree when they are ripe. They only fall off on their own when they have lost quite a lot of their original weight. Coconuts only really pose a danger to the people that pick them. They knock the fruit off the trees using long sticks. This can cause the coconuts to fall unpredictably, potentially injuring the person below.

The idea that coconuts are responsible for so many deaths actually started with a study by Dr Peter Barss on the number of coconut injuries reported to one hospital in Papua New Guinea. In four years only five people were killed by coconut trees and this included people falling out of them and trees falling down in storms, as well as falling coconuts. His research has been misused by people to claim that dozens of people in the world are killed by coconuts each year. This would assume that everybody lived on tropical islands covered in coconut trees, which unfortunately is not the case.

# Summer is WARM because we are closer to the Sun

This claim makes a lot of sense. When the Earth passes closer to the Sun, it's hotter.

## BUT THAT'S ACTUALLY NOT WHY SUMMER IS WARM.

The path of the Earth's orbit around the Sun is not quite a perfect circle. It is slightly oval in shape with the Sun just off-centre. As a result, the planet is closer to the Sun at one time of year – in January. January, for people who live in the northern hemisphere, is in the middle of winter. In London, Paris and New York, it is cold – and everyone is wearing mittens when the Earth is closest to the Sun.

The reason we get warm summers and cold winters is to do with the fact that the Earth is tilted. If it wasn't tilted, the Sun would be pointing straight at the equator (the Earth's middle) all the time. But because of the tilt, as we orbit the Sun, it shines on different bits of the planet for longer at different times of year.

In June, the Sun shines on the northern hemisphere for longer. Daytime lasts from 4 o'clock in the morning until after 10 o'clock at night – warming everything up for over 18 hours. In January, the Sun rises much later and sets much earlier – cutting the hours of daylight to just eight hours or so.

In the southern hemisphere, this is reversed, with longer days in January and shorter ones in June. So it is summer there when it is winter in the north.

Earth's wonky orbit does make a very slight difference, however. Because we are a little bit closer to the Sun in January, the summers in the southern hemisphere are a little bit warmer than they are in the north, and the winters down south are a little bit colder. But the main reason that summers are warm is not because we are closer to the Sun, but because we are facing towards it for longer each day.

# Lightning NEVER strikes in the same place twice

This popular saying is meant to put people's minds at rest when something bad has happened to them. It reassures them that something bad can't happen to the same person twice.

## SHOULD PEOPLE BE REASSURED BY THIS?

# DOES LIGHTNING REALLY NOT STRIKE IN THE SAME PLACE TWICE?

Unfortunately, lightning can strike in the same place twice. A lot of the time we want it to — we build some of our tall buildings in such a way that they attract lightning.

**WHY WOULD PEOPLE WANT TO ATTRACT LIGHTNING?**

Lightning will often strike the tallest thing in the immediate area. Very tall buildings, like the Empire State building in New York City, get hit by lightning dozens of times every year. Lightning can do a lot of damage — destroying roofs and starting fires. To avoid this damage, tall buildings have lightning rods. The rods attract bolts of lightning and give them a path to travel along to reach the ground.

Lightning rods were invented in 1752 by the famous American statesman and inventor, Benjamin Franklin. Franklin did a lot of work to prove that lightning was actually electricity. He attached a rod (made of metal attached to an electrical wire) to his chimney. He ran the wire all the way down the house to the ground. To this he attached an electric bell. Every time the rod was struck by lightning, the bell would ring, proving that there was electricity passing from the top of the rod down through the wire to the ground, ringing the bell as it went.

Unfortunately, people on golf courses get hit by lightning very often. If a storm has gathered and lightning is ready to strike, someone out in the open, swinging a metal golf club or holding a metal umbrella, is behaving like a lightning rod. So don't play golf in a storm.

If you are outside when a storm hits, squat close to the ground, and keep away from tall objects like trees — especially if the trees are the only tall objects in the area.

So, the popular saying should be, 'Stand in the open with an umbrella during a storm and there is a good chance lightning will strike you. Stand there again next time there's a storm, and there's a good chance lightning will strike twice in the same place!'

# Hares are MAD especially in March

The March Hare and the Mad Hatter are famously crazy characters from the *Alice in Wonderland* stories by Lewis Carroll. However, the reputation of hares going a little loopy in the month of March goes way beyond Wonderland.

Hares are energetic creatures all year round. The brown hare is among the fastest land animals around, with a top speed of up to 70 kilometres per hour. Speed is the hare's greatest defence against predators, and young hares will practise tearing around the fields from an early age.

However, in March (and the rest of the months in spring) hares can be spotted chasing each other, leaping in the air, and standing on their hind legs and boxing each other. It is this behaviour that has led to the expression 'as mad as a March hare' — a phrase that has been around for at least 500 years.

The truth is that spring is breeding season for hares. Male hares get very protective of their territory and become aggressive towards other males who might want to steal away female hares in the area. Hares will stand on their back legs to look dangerous and even box their opponents. Moreover, any female hare, called a doe, who doesn't want the attentions of a male, will let him know by thumping him repeatedly until he gets the message.

MAD? NO. JUST YOUNG AND IN LOVE — OR RATHER, YOUNG AND NOT INTERESTED IN LOVE IN THE SLIGHTEST!

As for the Mad Hatter ... the reputation of milliners (people who make hats) behaving strangely may have sound reasoning behind it. People who made hats 200 years ago worked with several dangerous chemicals, including mercury, which is highly toxic. Over time, the effects of poisoning from these chemicals could indeed damage a person's brain. For this reason, some milliners of old really were a little crazy.

# Ostriches hide their HEADS in the sand

Do you remember being very young and thinking that if you closed your eyes as tightly as possible you would be invisible – the theory being that people can't see you if you can't see them?

A lot of people believe that ostriches are very stupid animals. So it is not unreasonable to conclude that ostriches bury their heads in the sand when they sense danger because they think that if their pea-brained heads are covered they will be completely invisible to a hungry hyena.

Ostriches have been accused of being stupid for a long time. The Romans kept them for food and were amazed by their agility and strength. Roman citizens enjoyed watching fights between ostriches and gladiators. Two thousand years ago, the Ancient Roman writer and scientist Pliny the Elder wrote that ostriches 'imagine, when they have thrust their head and neck into a bush, that the whole of their body is concealed.' But is it true?

No. Ostriches are quite stupid as animals go. Their brains are smaller than their eyeballs. However, they are not stupid enough to bury their heads in the sand. If they did, they would probably die from suffocation or be eaten, whichever came first.

Ostriches have a number of options when they are scared by an approaching predator. They can run away at over 65 kilometres per hour. They can kick the predator – ostriches have a kick hard enough to break a man's leg. They can also hide from the predator, lying flat on the ground, resembling a bush.

The idea that ostriches bury their heads in the sand could come from the fact that male ostriches dig holes as nests in which to conceal the eggs in the sparse landscape. These holes can be up to 50 centimetres deep. Ostriches tending to their eggs would also look like they had their heads buried in the ground.

Another reason for the myth might be due to the fact that ostriches eat grit and small stones. These help them grind up food to make it easier to digest. The sight of ostriches chewing away at the ground with their beaks may have given people the impression that the big, dumb, scared birds were trying to bury their heads.

# The WORST thing for your teeth is eating sweets

For a hundred years, children have been told that sugar rots their teeth, and that eating sweets will lead them to the dentist's chair.

Recent research shows that sugar might not be the cavity-causing villain people once thought it was. As far as your teeth are concerned, there are much worse things you can eat — stickier things that will cling to your teeth, giving bacteria longer to attack the hard enamel coating of your teeth.

Some scientists now believe that 'simple carbohydrates', otherwise known as sugars, are easily washed away from teeth by normal saliva. Complex carbohydrates are not. These complex carbohydrates include the starch and fibre found in bread, cereal and pasta.

Boiled sweets, chocolate and fudge are not the worst things you can eat if you don't want cavities. Crisps, crackers and cereal are.

And, obvious as it sounds, your chances of keeping shiny, healthy teeth into your old age are increased dramatically if you brush after each meal and floss regularly.

# Camels store water in their HUMPS

Everyone knows that the reason camels trek across desert sands, surviving for days without a drink of water is because they keep a handy supply of water stored in their humps. Right?

No. It is true that camels are highly suited to life in a desert where water is scarce. They can survive extreme temperatures — searing heat and bitter cold — and they can indeed go for long periods of time without drinking water.

WATER

Dehydration — when the body loses water — is one of the biggest dangers an animal can face in the desert. A human being in the desert without water will die after only a few days. Human beings lose weight through water loss and losing just 20 per cent of their body weight in water will usually prove fatal. A camel, on the other hand, can lose up to 30 per cent with no ill effects.

However, while a camel's hump (or humps — some camels have two) are used for storing emergency supplies, it is not water that is stored there. A camel's hump is made of fat, which its body uses when food is hard to come by.

Keeping all its fat in its hump means a camel has little fat on the rest of its body. This is useful, because a camel that was fat all over would sweat in the desert heat, and sweating means losing water. Camels also have a remarkable ability to raise and lower their body temperature depending on how hot the Sun is. They can conserve energy, and again, keep sweating to a minimum.

As long as a camel gets some green vegetation to eat, and a little dew to lick off plants in the morning, it can go for several months without a proper drink. When it finally does reach water, it makes up for lost time by consuming up to 50 gallons (200 litres) at once! Camels aren't fussy either — water that is stagnant or salty and would make a human very ill is OK for camels.

So where does the camel keep 50 gallons of water? The answer is all over. The camel absorbs water into its body fluids, including into its blood. Absorbing large amounts of water into the blood would kill a person pretty much instantly, but it is not a problem for a camel.

You can see why people who live and travel in desert regions rely so heavily on camels for transport, and why these animals are known around the Sahara as 'Ata Allah', or 'The Gift From God'.

# RATS are filthy creatures

Rats have a very bad reputation — they eat rubbish, live in sewers and were responsible for the bubonic plague.

IT'S HARD TO LOVE A RAT.

But wait ... did you know that rats love to play together and will look after injured and sick rats until they are well again? They love company, and get really lonely if they get separated from their friends. They will even look after each other's babies.

Experts believe that rats are smart — smarter than mice, guinea pigs and rabbits. In tests they have proved that rats can remember complicated routes to places where there might be a regular source of food or water.

The truth is rats are extremely clean, as animals go. They groom themselves and each other for hours each day. Moreover, they like to keep their homes clean and tidy, too.

Rats do carry a disease transmitted via their urine, known as 'Weil's disease', (pronounced 'viles'). This disease is picked up most often on river banks or in muddy ditches, so be careful when playing near rivers or lakes, as it can cause fever in humans.

So what about the plague? Bubonic plague is caused by bacteria. The bacteria live on fleas, and yes, fleas do like to live on rats, but they also get on to cats and dogs and people. In 1665, when plague struck London, the city was filthy. There were open sewers in the streets and people shared their homes with farm animals. The conditions were perfect for the disease to spread, but rats were probably less likely than cats or dogs to carry the disease.

So why do rats have a reputation for loving filth? That is the fault of untidy humans. Rats are attracted to the filthy places where food and rubbish are left lying around by people.

IN REALITY, RATS ARE CLEANING UP OUR MESS!

# Dogs only wag their tails when they are HAPPY

Now we all know that happy dogs wag their tails. You only have to say the 'w' of 'walkies' to set an expectant pooch's excitable tail wagging. However, it's not true to claim happy dogs always wag their tails or that unhappy dogs don't. Tail-wagging is just a part of doggy body language, and can mean many different things.

A wagging tail is generally a sign of excitement. The faster it wags, the more excited the dog is. But this excitement isn't always happiness. You have to look at other body language to work out whether the excitement is happy or angry. Generally speaking, a low tail position indicates a relaxed dog.

When a dog's tail is held low and slowly swinging, this indicates contentment. A high tail, or one held curving forwards over a dog's back, can indicate aggression. If a dog's tail is wagging fast in this position, you may have an excited and aggressive dog.

Dogs use tail-wagging to communicate. If you put a bowl of food in front of a hungry dog, it will wag its tail, showing excitement and pleasure and maybe even to say 'thank you'. But if the dog discovers a bowl of food on the floor when there is no one there to see, it might be delighted and excited, but it won't wag his tail.

Very young puppies don't wag their tails, even though they are physically capable of doing it. They spend a lot of time lying around and eating, and don't really notice too much what's going on around them. It is only when puppies start to play that they start to learn to use dog language. For example, a puppy might learn that if it nips one of its puppy pals while wagging its tail, its pal will know it is only kidding and won't want to start a fight.

SO, A WAGGY DOG IS NOT ALWAYS A HAPPY DOG, AND A DOG ONLY WAGS WHEN SOMEONE IS WATCHING.

*Do Elephants Ever Forget?*
ISBN: 978-1-78055-512-6